Need For Speed
BIKES

JAMES GIBB

Published in 2009 by TAJ Books International LLP

27, Ferndown Gardens,
Cobham,
Surrey,
UK,
KT11 2BH

www.tajbooks.com

ISBN-13: 978-1-84406-135-8

Printed in China.

Need For Speed

BIKES

JAMES GIBB

T&J

Hildebrand & Wolfmüller of 1894

The modern motorcycle is descended from the pedal cycle. Its origins are lost in the mists of time, but it is generally acknowledged to have been invented by the German Karl von Drais in about 1817. This was a very basic machine propelled by pushing it along with ones feet. In 1840 a Scottish blacksmith Kirkpatrick MacMillan made a machine with pedals and cranks. Subsequently Pierre Michaux in France designed the "Velocipede" which had pedals attached to the front wheel.

John Kemp Starley an Englishman manufactured in 1885 what is regarded as the modern bicycle with gears and a chain drive and brakes of course. It is from this that the motorcycle as we know it today derived. Early machines were basically bicycles with a small motor inserted in the frame. The first of these was made by Gottlieb Daimler and Wilhelm Maybach in Bad Cannstatt, Stuttgart in 1885. They named it the Reitwagen (Riding Car). However an American, Sylvester Howard Roper had demonstrated a steam driven two wheel vehicle at fairs and circuses in 1867.

Neither of the above were sold to the public. The first put on sale was made by Hildebrand and Wolfmuller in 1894. The other major development was the invention of the pneumatic tyre by John Boyd Dunlop in 1888. All the ingredients were now available leading to the birth of the mass-produced motorcycle, frame, seat, pneumatic tyres and a method of transmission of mechanical propulsion.

EarlyDays

Up to the beginning of the first world war Indian in the United States was the major producer of motor cycles, with production peaking at 20,000 a year. By 1920 Harley-Davidson had assumed the lead with dealers in 67 countries. In 1928 the German maker DKW had taken over as the largest manufacturer. After the second world war the British BSA Group had the lead producing 75,000 machines a year until 1955. The German NSU Motorenwerke was the worlds major manufacturer until the 1970s. The Japanese makers Honda, Suzuki, Yamaha and Kawasaki then assumed the mantle of mass manufacture, although Harley-Davidson, Triumph, MotoGuzzi still maintain a major presence in the niche market.

The Mechanics

The technical specification of the motorcycle has not changed in its 100 year history. A metal frame made from steel tube supports front and rear forks, these were originally unsprung, but eventually the front forks were independently sprung with friction dampers which were adjustable. This led to telescopic forks with internal oil dampers. The rear independent suspension followed soon after.

The brakes were of the drum variety similar to those on motor cars, but because of the restrictions on the size of these they were not as effective as one would expect for the speeds attained by the machine. The calliper disc brake became universal after its introduction on cars.

Engines on the early machines were usually of a small capacity and single cylinder, with notable exceptions by Indian and Harley-Davidson who had twin-cylinder V configuration and Ariel who had a square four layout. These engines were side-valves operated by push-rods open to the elements extremely noisy and distributing oil over the riders. Most of these engines were air-cooled but some makers such as Scott had water-cooled installations, which were quieter and cleaner.

The engines had vertical cylinders, but Douglas developed the flat-twin very successfully, with BMW eventually designing a similar concept. The engines were principally made from cast-iron with crank-cases of aluminium. The pistons originally made from iron changed to

1st Daimler Motorcycle made in 1885

INTRODUCTION

In June 1919, Ralph Hepburn came to national prominence when he won the 200-mile (320 km) National Championship at Ascot Park in Los Angeles driving for the Harley-Davidson factory.

handlebars. Gears were non-existent on the very early machines. Then a separate gearbox driven by an adjustable chain from the engine was fitted. The most notable of these was the "Burman" originally with three speeds. Early machines had hand change mechanisms, these eventually developed into the foot change we are familiar with today. The original transmission was by belt on pulleys, this changed to gears driving a roller chain to the back wheel, the tension was adjusted by altering the wheel whose spindle was located in slots in the rear frame

The first machines were started by being pushed by the rider, kick-starts were then introduced, together with a hand operated device to decompress the engine to enable easy starting. Speed indication was obtained by handle-bar mounted speedometer, which on more expensive machines was augmented by a revolution counter. An ampere meter was also mounted to indicate battery state.

Prior to batteries being installed lighting was by acetylene lamps, each lamp had a reservoir containing carbide and water generating gas, this was fed through a jet which was ignited by the rider. A method of warning of approach developed from the bulb operated horn to the electric type in use today.

Modern Developments

Post second world war saw the major developments that are recognisable in today's machines.

Engines have become highly sophisticated, being multi-cylindered with overhead camshafts a common trend. Synthetic oils have been developed to cope with increases in temperatures and loads within the engine. Gearboxes are now integral with the engine, sharing the same lubricants. Four and five speed ratios are common. Transmissions are by technically advanced roller chain with each roller sealed containing a lubricant. A shaft drive like the design introduced by BMW is more common, which is also used by MotoGuzzi.

Wheels which were for many years spoked, are now more commonly die-cast aluminium. Brakes are disc with hydraulic cylinders and extremely efficient. Frames are stiffer, with suspension front and rear having adjustable hydraulic damping. Lighting has been improved beyond all recognition particularly with the introduction of quartz halogen bulbs. Tyres are designed to deal with wet conditions, enabling higher speeds without mishap. Many machines have fairings to protect the rider from the worst of the weather, but also leading to improved fuel economy.

aluminium, while the valves were made from steel alloys. Lubrication was originally by vegetable derived oils but, became mineral based eventually. Ignition was by magneto to a spark plug with eventually a circuit breaker and coil was introduced. Fuel was by a carburetor with a float in a chamber under a gravity-fed tank, jets then introduced the fuel to the engine by an inlet manifold. Exhaust was into a pipe leading to a silencer exhausting at the rear of the machine. Two valves per cylinder was the norm.

Clutches were leather based initially but developed into cork and asbestos faced plates. This developed into the all-metal clutch which serves today. They were controlled by a hand-operated lever on the

Modern Manufacturers

Harley-Davidson can probably claim to be the longest US manufacturer in continual production. Triumph have been around for about eighty years but not in continuous production. The Japanese makers have been around longer than most people realise, Kawasaki being part of a large engineering conglomerate, Yamaha having its origins in musical instrument manufacture. The German company BMW built aircraft engines and cars before moving into the motorcycle field.

Moto Guzzi were made before the war and had a very good reputation in road racing after it. Husqvarna in Sweden have been made since 1903 so may claim to have been around longer than Harley-Davidson.

AJS 1910-1974

AJS was the name used for cars and motorcycles made by the Wolverhampton, England company A. J. Stevens & Co. Ltd, from 1909 to 1931, by then holding 117 motorcycle world records, and after the firm was sold the name continued to be used by Matchless, Associated Motorcycles and Norton-Villiers on four-stroke motorcycles till 1969, and since the names resale in 1974, on small capacity two-strokes.

Brough Superior 1920-1940

Brough Superior motorcycles and motor cars were made by George Brough in his Brough Superior works on Haydn Road in Nottingham, England from 1919 to 1940. They were dubbed the "Rolls-Royce of Motorcycles" by H. D. Teague of The Motorcycle newspaper. Approximately 3048 of 19 models were made in 21 years of production. In 2004, around 1000 still exist. T.E. Lawrence ("Lawrence of Arabia") owned seven bikes and died from injuries sustained while crashing one. George Bernard Shaw was another among many celebrities that were enthusiastic about Brough products.

BSA 1910-1973

BSA was founded in 1861 in the Gun Quarter, Birmingham, England by fourteen gunsmiths of the Birmingham Small Arms Trade Association, who had together supplied arms to the British government during the Crimean War. The company branched out as the gun trade declined; in the 1870s they manufactured the Otto Dicycle, in the 1880s the company began to manufacture bicycles and in 1903 the company's first experimental motorcycle was constructed. Their first prototype automobile was produced in 1907 and the next year the company sold 150 automobiles. By 1909 they were offering a number of motorcycles for sale and in 1910 BSA purchased the British Daimler Company for its

A 1913 Fabrique National in-line four with shaft drive from Belgium.

automobile engines.

The first wholly BSA motorcycles were built in 1910, before then engines had come from other manufacturers. BSA Motorcycles Ltd was set up as a subsidiary in 1919. Initially, after World War II, BSA motorcycles were not generally seen as racing machines, compared to the likes of Norton. . In the immediate post war period few were entered in races such as the TT races, though this changed dramatically in the Junior Clubman event (smaller engine motorcycles racing over some 3 or 4 laps around one of the Isle of Man courses). In 1947 there were but a couple of BSA mounted riders, but by 1952 BSA were in the majority and in 1956 the makeup was 53 BSA, 1 Norton and 1 Velocette.

To improve US sales, in 1954, for example, BSA entered a team of riders in the 200 mile Daytona beach race with a mixture of single cylinder Gold Stars and twin cylinder Shooting Stars assembled by Roland Pike. The BSA team riders amazingly took first, second, third, fourth, and fifth places with two more riders finishing at 8th and 16th. This was the first case of a one brand sweep.

FN

FN (Fabrique Nationale de Herstal) was a Belgian company established in 1899 to make arms and ammunition, and from 1901 to 1967 was also a motorcycle manufacturer. FN manufactured the world's first four cylinder motorcycle, was famous for the use of shaft drive in all models from 1903 to 1923, achieved success in sprint and long distance motorcycle racing, and after 1945, also in motocross.

In 1899 FN made shaft and chain driven bicycles, and in 1900 experimented with a clip-on engine. In December 1901 the first 133 cc single cylinder motorcycle was built, followed in 1903 by a shaft driven 188 cc single cylinder motorcycle. In 1904 a 300 cc single cylinder motorcycle was produced. In 1909 the two speed singles had camshafts to open the inlets, instead of the earlier "automatic" valves. Starting from 1912 the singles had a hand lever clutch and foot pedal rear brake.

The FN Four

In 1905 the first 362 cc shaft drive in-line FN inlet-over-exhaust four cylinder motorcycle appeared, designed by Paul Kelecom. This was the world's first manufactured four cylinder motorcycle. By 1907 the Four engine had grown to 412 cc, and that year's single cylinder 244 cc FN motorcycle was the first bike with a multiple ratio belt drive system, using a patented variable size engine pulley. For 1908, the US Export model began manufacture. The Four had a 493 cc engine, and in 1910 that became 498 cc. This bike weighed 75 kg (165 lb) dry, and could do 40 mph (64 km/h). The 1913 Fours had a two speed gearbox and clutch, at the rear of the shaft drive, and bicycle pedals were permanently replaced with footrests from then on. For 1914 the FN "Type 700" 748 cc Four was released, with the gearbox at the rear of the engine.

Husqvarna

As with many motorcycle manufacturers, Husqvarna first began producing bicycles in the late 19th century. In 1903, they made the jump to motorcycle manufacturing. In 1920 Husqvarna established its own engine factory and the first engine to be designed was a 550 cc four-stroke 50-degree side-valve V-twin engine, similar to those made by companies like Harley-Davidson and Indian. Although they once made motorcycles for street use, and raced at road circuits such as the Isle of Man TT prior to World War II, they are more well known for producing world championship winning motocross and enduro bikes. In the 1960s, their lightweight, two-stroke engined off-road bikes helped make the once dominant British four-stroke motorcycles obsolete. Throughout the 1960s and 1970s they were a dominant force in the motocross world, winning 14 Motocross world championships in the 125cc, 250cc and 500cc divisions and 24 enduro world championships.

The Husqvarna motorcycle division was sold to Italian motorcycle manufacturer Cagiva in 1987 and became part of MV Agusta Motor S.p.A. The motorcycles (widely known as a "Husky") are now produced in Varese. Husqvarna produces a diverse range of motocross, enduro and supermoto machines using their own two-stroke or four-stroke engines, ranging in capacity from 125cc to 576cc. Racing continues to be important to Husqvarna, competing in world enduro and world supermoto championships. Gerald Delepine, riding a Husqvarna

SMR660, became supermoto world champion in 2005.

In July 2007 Husqvarna was purchased by BMW for a reported 93 million euros. BMW Motorrad plans to continue operating Husqvarna Motorcycles as a separate enterprise. All development, sales and production activities, as well as the current workforce, will remain in place at its present location at Varese.

Royal Enfield 1899-1970 (UK)

Royal Enfield was the brand of the Enfield Cycle Company, an English engineering company. Most famous for producing motorcycles, they also produced, bicycles, lawnmowers, stationary engines, and even rifle parts for the Royal Small Arms Factory in Enfield. This legacy of weapons manufacture is reflected in the logo, a cannon, and their motto "Made like a gun, goes like a bullet". It also enabled the use of the brand name Royal Enfield from 1890.

In 1955 Enfield of India started assembling Bullet motorcycles under licence from UK components, and by 1962 were manufacturing complete bikes. The original Redditch, Worcestershire - based company dissolved in 1970, but Enfield of India, based in Chennai, continued, and bought the rights to the Royal Enfield name in 1995. Royal Enfield production continues, and now Royal Enfield is considered as the oldest motorcycle company in the world still in production.

Sunbeam 1912-1957

Sunbeam was a British motorcycle marque generally known for high qualityJohn Marston, the man who started it all was born in Ludlow, Shropshire, U.K. in 1836, of a minor landowning family. In 1851 at age 15, he was sent to Wolverhampton to be apprenticed to Edward Perry as a japanware manufacturer. At the age of 23 he left and set up his own japanning business, John Marston Ltd, making any and every sort of domestic article. He did so well that when Perry died in 1871, Marston took over his company and incorporated it in his own.

The company began making bicycles, and on the suggestion of his wife Ellen, Marston adopted the trademark brand "Sunbeam". Consequently, the Paul Street works were called Sunbeamland. John Marston was a perfectionist, and this was reflected in the high build quality of the Sunbeam bicycle, which had an enclosure around the chain in which an oil bath kept the chain lubricated and clean. They were made until 1936, and to the end remained the best bicycle money could buy.From 1903 John Marston Ltd had made some early experiments in adding engines to bicycles but they were unsuccessful, one man being killed. John Marston's aversion to motorcycles did not encourage

A 1935 Indian Four.

further development, and so the Sunbeam Motor Car Company Ltd was founded in 1905. However, suffering from a slump which hit car making, Marston was pushed into making motorcycles from 1912 onwards (at the age of 76), for which there was a greater and increasing market. Following in the tradition of their bicycles, the motorcycles were of high-quality, usually with a single cylinder, and known as the "Gentleman's Machine." Sunbeam motorcycles performed well in the early days of the famous TT (Tourist Trophy) races in the Isle of Man.

After the First World War, the Marston company was sold to a consortium. In 1919 the consortium became part of Nobel Industries Limited. In 1927 Nobel Industries amalgamated with Brunner Mond Ltd. to form Imperial Chemical Industries (ICI). In this huge organization motorcycles were a small part.

In 1937 the Sunbeam motorcycle trademark was sold to Associated Motor Cycles Ltd ("AMC"), which continued to make Sunbeam bicycles and motorcycles until 1939. Other brandnames of motorcycles owned by AMC were Matchless, AJS, Norton, James, and Francis-Barnett.

In 1943, AMC sold the Sunbeam name to BSA, and Sunbeam Cycles Ltd came into being. Three Sunbeam motorcycle models were produced from 1946 to 1956, not in the main BSA factory at Small Heath, Birmingham, but in Redditch, Worcestershire. These were followed by two scooter models from 1959-1964. The new Sunbeam motorcycles were of an entirely new design inspired by BMW German army motorcycles captured in World War II.

Velocette 1909-1971

Velocette is the name given to motorcycles that were made by Veloce Ltd, in Hall Green, Birmingham, England. One of several motorcycle manufacturers in Birmingham, Velocette was a small, family-owned firm, selling far fewer hand-built motorcycles than the giant BSA, Norton, or Triumph concerns. Renowned for the quality of their products, the company was 'always in the picture' in international motorcycle racing, from the mid-1920s through the 1950s, culminating in two world championship titles (1949–1950 350 cc) and their legendary and still-unbeaten 24 hours at 100 mph (161 km/h) record. Veloce, while small, was a great technical innovator and many of their patented designs are commonplace on motorcycles today, including the positive-stop foot shift and swingarm rear fork with hydraulic shocks The company was founded by John Taylor (born Johannes Gütgemann and later known as John Goodman), and William Gue as "Taylor, Gue Ltd." in 1905. Their first motorcycle was the Veloce. Later that year, John Taylor set up Veloce Limited, to produce cycles and related products and services. Veloce Ltd initially produced four-stroke motorcycles. The first two-stroke, built in 1913, was called a Velocette. This name was used for all of their subsequent models.

Vincent-HRD 1928-1955

HRD was founded by the British (RFC) pilot, Howard Raymond Davies, who was shot down and captured by the Germans in 1917. Legend has it that it was while a prisoner of war that he conceived the idea of building his own motorcycle, and contemplated how he might achieve that. It was not until 1924 that Davies entered into partnership with E J Massey, trading as HRD Motors. Various models were produced, generally powered by JAP (J A Prestwich) engines.

Unfortunately, even though HRD motorcycles won races the company ran at a loss, and in January 1928 it went into voluntary liquidation. The company was initially bought by Ernest Humphries of OK-Supreme Motors for the factory space, and the HRD name, jigs, tools, patterns, and remaining components were subsequently offered for sale again.

Indian 1901-1953

The Indian Motocycle Manufacturing Company (sic) was a motorcycle manufacturer in Springfield, Massachusetts. Indian was America's oldest motorcycle brand and was once the largest manufacturer of motorcycles in the world. The most popular models were the Scout, made prior to WWII, and the Chief, which had its heyday from 1922-53

INTRODUCTION

Harley-Davidson 1903-

Harley-Davidson Motor Company is an American manufacturer of motorcycles based in Milwaukee, Wisconsin. The company sells heavyweight (over 750 cc) motorcycles designed for cruising on the highway. Harley-Davidson motorcycles (popularly known as "Harleys") have a distinctive design and exhaust note. They are especially noted for the tradition of heavy customization that gave rise to the chopper-style of motorcycle.

Harley-Davidson attracts a loyal brand community, with licensing of the Harley-Davidson logo accounting for almost 5% of the company's net revenue ($41 million in 2004). In 2003, the Buell Motorcycle Company became a wholly-owned subsidiary of Harley-Davidson, the same year that the Motor Company celebrated its 100th birthday. The Motor Company supplies many American police forces with their motorcycle fleets.

MotoGuzzi 1921-

Moto Guzzi (aka "Guzzi") is an Italian motorcycle manufacturer that has endured from the industry's infancy to its place today as the oldest European manufacturer in continuous motorcycle production. Guzzi is now one of seven brands owned by Piaggio & Co. SpA, Europe's largest motorcycle manufacturer and the world's fourth largest motorcycle manufacturer by unit sales.

Established in 1921 in Mandello del Lario, Italy, Moto Guzzi has led Italy's motorcycling manufacture, enjoyed prominence in world-wide motorcycle racing, and led the industry in ground-breaking innovation — for the greater part of its history.

Today Moto Guzzi impresses its heritage on a range of motorcycles in touring, cruising, racing and naked configurations — each with the company's iconic, air-cooled 90° V-twin engines.

The Dyna line of motorcycles debuts with the 1991 FXDB Dyna Glide Sturgis

Gilera 1909-

Gilera is an Italian motorcycle manufacturer founded in Arcore in 1909 by Giuseppe Gilera. In 1969 the company was purchased by the Piaggio & Co. SpA -- which now holds six marques and is the world's fourth largest motorcycle manufacturer.

In 1935 Gilera acquired rights to the Rondine four-cylinder engine. This formed the basis for Gileras racing machines for nearly forty years. From the mid-thirties Gilera developed a range of four-stroke engine machines. The engines ranged from 100 to 500cc. The most famous of which was the 1939 Saturno.

After World War II, Gilera dominated Grand Prix motorcycle racing, winning the 500cc road racing world championship 6 times in 8 years. Facing a downturn in motorcycle sales due to the increase in the popularity of automobiles after the war, Gilera made a gentleman's agreement with the other Italian motorcycle makers to quit Grand Prix racing after the 1957 season as a cost cutting measure. In 1992, Gilera made a return to the Grand Prix arena and Piaggio continues to produce small-displacement motorcycles with the Gilera name.

Honda 1938-

Honda's first motorcycle to be put on sale was the 1947 A-Type (one year before the company was officially founded). However, Honda's first full-fledged motorcycle on the market was the 1949 Dream D-Type. It was equipped with a 98cc engine producing around 3 horsepower (2.2 kW). This was followed by other highly popular scooters throughout the 1950s.

In 1958, the American Honda Company was founded and one year later, Honda introduced its first model in the United States, the 1959 Honda C100 Super Cub. The Honda Cub holds the title of being the best-selling vehicle in history, with around 50 million units sold around the world.

1954 Gilera 150 Sport

INTRODUCTION

Kawasaki 1953-

Kawasaki Heavy Industries Consumer Products and Machinery Company is the Consumer Products and Machinery production division of Kawasaki Heavy Industries. It produces Motorcycles, ATVs, Utility vehicles, Jet Ski personal watercrafts, General-purpose gasoline engines.

Kawasaki's Aircraft Company began the development of a motorcycle engine in 1949. The development was completed in 1952 and mass production started in 1953. The engine was an air-cooled, 148cc, OHV, 4-stroke single cylinder with a maximum power of 4 PS (3.9 hp/2.9 kW) at 4,000 rpm. In 1954 the first complete Kawasaki Motorcycle was produced under the name of Meihatsu, a subsidiary of Kawasaki Aircraft. In 1960 Kawasaki completed construction of a factory dedicated exclusively to motorcycle production and bought Meguro Motorcycles. Kawasaki has since then become one of the world's major motorcycle manufacturers.

Suzuki 1909-

In 1909, Michio Suzuki founded the Suzuki Loom Company in the small seacoast village of Hamamatsu, Japan. Business boomed as Suzuki built weaving looms for Japan's giant silk industry. Suzuki's only desire was to build better, more user-friendly looms. In 1929, Michio Suzuki invented a new type of weaving machine, which was exported overseas. Suzuki filed as many as 120 patents and utility model rights. For the first 30 years of the company's existence, its focus was on the development and production of these exceptionally complex machines.

But the joy was short-lived as the cotton market collapsed in 1951.

Faced with this colossal challenge, Suzuki's thoughts went back to motor vehicles. After the war, the Japanese had a great need for affordable, reliable personal transportation. A number of firms began offering "clip-on" gas-powered engines that could be attached to the typical bicycle. Suzuki's first two-wheel ingenuity came in the form of a motorized bicycle called, the "Power Free." Designed to be inexpensive and simple to build and maintain, the 1952 Power Free featured a 36 cc two-stroke engine. An unprecedented feature was the double-sprocket gear system, enabling the rider to either pedal with the engine assisting, pedal without engine assist, or simply disconnect the pedals and run on engine power alone. The system was so ingenious that the patent office of the new democratic government granted Suzuki a financial subsidy to continue research in motorcycle engineering, and so was born Suzuki Motor Corporation.

In 1953, Suzuki scored the first of countless racing victories when the tiny 60 cc "Diamond Free" won its class in the Mount Fuji Hill Climb.

By 1954, Suzuki was producing 6,000 motorcycles per month and had officially changed its name to Suzuki Motor Co., Ltd. Following the success of its first motorcycles, Suzuki created an even more successful automobile: the 1955 Suzulight. Suzuki showcased its penchant for innovation from the beginning. The Suzulight included front-wheel drive, four-wheel independent suspension and rack-and-pinion steering -- features common on cars half a century later.

Yamaha 1955-

Yamaha Motor Company Limited, a Japanese motorized vehicle-producing company (whose HQ is at 2500 Shingai, Iwata, Shizuoka), is part of the Yamaha Corporation. After expanding Yamaha Corporation into the world's biggest piano maker, then Yamaha CEO Genichi Kawakami took Yamaha into the field of motorized vehicles on July 1, 1955. The company's intensive research into metal alloys for use in acoustic pianos had given Yamaha wide knowledge of the making of lightweight, yet sturdy and reliable metal constructions. This knowledge was easily applied to the making of metal frames and motor parts for motorcycles. Yamaha Motor is the world's second largest producer of motorcycles. It also produces many other motorized vehicles such as all-terrain vehicles, boats, snowmobiles, outboard motors, and personal watercraft.

BMW 1923-

BMW Motorrad, a subsidiary of BMW, manufactures motorcycles. Originally an aircraft engine manufacturer at the turn of the last century and through World War I, BMW introduced the first motorcycle under its name, the R32, in 1923. Although BMW motorcycles have been long associated with their original engine configuration, the flat-twin or boxer engine, the company today manufactures a full line of motorcycles in a variety of engine and riding configurations

BMW began as an aircraft engine manufacturer before World War I. With the Armistice, the Treaty of Versailles banned any German air force and thus need for aero engines, so the company turned first to making air brakes, agricultural machinery, toolboxes and office furniture. Dissatisfied with that, they eventually turned to manufacturing

29 BMW WR 750

motorcycles. After the MB215 engine and the two stroke "Flink", 1923 saw the arrival of a complete motorcycle under the BMW name, the R 32.

Max Friz, BMW's chief designer, turned to motorcycle and car engines. Within four weeks, he had copied the now-legendary opposing flat twin cylinder engine which we know today as the boxer engine. This product was the second revolutionary product that Friz copied that firmly placed BMW AG in a profitable position.

The first boxer engine was the fore-and-aft M2B15, based on a British Douglas design. It was manufactured by BMW in 1921–1922 but mostly used in other brands of motorcycles, notably Victoria of Nuremberg. The M2B15 proved to be moderately successful and BMW used it in its own Helios motorcycle. BMW also developed and manufactured a small 2-stroke motorcycle called the Flink for a short time.

DKW 1919-1958

Dampf Kraft Wagen (German: steam-driven car) or DKW is a historic car and motorcycle marque. In 1916, the Danish engineer Jørgen Skafte Rasmussen founded a factory in Saxony, Germany, to produce steam fittings. In the same year, he attempted to produce a steam-driven car, called the DKW. Although unsuccessful, he made a two-stroke toy engine in 1919, called Des Knaben Wunsch — "a boy's desire". He also put a slightly modified version of this engine into a motorcycle and called it Das Kleine Wunder — "a little marvel". This was the real beginning of the DKW brand: by the 1930s, DKW was the world's largest motorcycle manufacturer.

In 1932, DKW merged with Audi, Horch and Wanderer to form the Auto Union. Auto Union came under Daimler-Benz ownership in 1957, and was finally purchased by the Volkswagen Group in 1964. The last DKW car was the F102 which ceased production in 1966; after this the brand was phased out.

NSU 1901-1958

NSU began as a knitting machine manufacturer in the town of Riedlingen on the Danube in 1873, and moved to Neckarsulm, where the river Sulm flows into the river Neckar, in 1884. The company soon began to produce bicycles as well, and by 1892, bicycle manufacturing had completely replaced the knitting machine production. At about this time, the name NSU (from Neckar and Sulm) appeared as brand name. In the early years of the 20th century NSU motorcycles were developed, in 1905 the first NSU cars appeared. In 1932 the car production in

Heilbronn was sold to Fiat. During World War II NSU designed and produced the famous Kettenkrad, NSU HK101 a half-tracked motorcycle with the engine of the Opel Olympia. After the war, NSU restarted in a completely destroyed plant with pre-war constructions like the Quick, OSL and Konsul motorbikes. And also still the HK101 could be purchased at NSU as an all terrain vehicle in a civil version. The first post war construction was the NSU Fox in 1949, available in a 2-stroke and a 4-stroke version. In 1953 the famous NSU Max followed, a 250 cc motorbike with a unique overhead camdrive with connecting rods. All these new models had a very innovative monocoque frame of pressed steel and a central rear suspension unit. Albert Roder, the genius chief engineer behind the success story, made it possible that in 1955 NSU became the biggest motorcycle producer in the world. NSU also holds 4 world records for speed: 1951, 1953, 1954 and 1955. In 1956 Wilhelm Herz started at the Bonneville Salt Flats, Utah. Herz was the first man to ride a motorcycle faster than 200 miles per hour, in August 1956. In 1957 NSU re-entered the car market with the new NSU Prinz, a small car with a doubled NSU Max engine, an air cooled two-cylinder engine of 600 cc and 20 hp. Motorbike production continued until 1968

The Sd. Kfz 2 Kleines Kettenkraftrad (Small-Tracked Motorcycle) was a light armored vehicle with the front end of a motorcycle attached to the rear end of a half-track. The handlebars operated differential brakes on the tracks as well as turning the front wheel. Powered by an 1500cc 4-cylinder Opel engine, it was produced by the thousands to equip Wehrmacht Panzer units.

Norton 1902-1999

Norton was a British motorcycle marque from Birmingham, founded in 1898 as a manufacturer of cycle chains.

By 1902 they had begun manufacturing motorcycles with bought-in engines. In 1908 a Norton built engine was added to the range. This began a long series of production of single cylinder motorcycles. They were one of the great names of the British motorcycle industry, producing machines which for decades dominated racing with highly tuned single cylinder engines under the Race Shop supremo Joe Craig.

Postwar a 500 cc twin cylinder model called the Dominator or Model 7 was added to the range for 1949, and this evolved into the 1970s through 500 cc, to 600 cc, to 650 cc, to 750 cc and to 850 cc models with the Dominator, 650, Atlas and Commando, all highly regarded road motorcycles of their time.

Norton F1 Rotary

APRILLIA RSV4

Aprilia RSV4 is a racing machine that, in line with the Aprilia tradition, follows a completely innovative approach in its design and construction. Its narrow V engine, the use of state-of-the-art electronics, plus its lightness and extreme compactness are only a few of the features that make it unique in the world. Aprilia RSV4 is designed and built with the same philosophy adopted by the Aprilia race division. This is why RSV4 is the most "complete" Superbike racing replica, ready for those who want to venture onto the track with a class leading motorcycle.

The engine of the RSV4 is the most innovative and powerful Aprilia has ever built. It is a super compact 999.6 cc 65° V-four cylinder engine designed for maximum power (180 CV), where powerplant engineering comes together with the finest materials and the most advanced electronic control solutions. Aprilia's engine, in fact, uses a Ride by Wire multimap technology, a solution that opens up new frontiers for engine management, with practically infinite possibilities for further development. In this latest RSV 1000 R, the V60 Magnesium engine is not only cleaner but even more powerful, confirming its reputation as the world's mightiest production twin. The modifications needed to achieve homologation to strict Euro 3 standards have not stopped Aprilia squeezing another 4 horsepower out of this amazing engine. The latest powerplant delivers 105.24 kW (143 HP) at the crank to push the bike to a top speed of over 280 km/h, aided by improved aerodynamics and even more efficient engine breathing.

APRILLIA DORSODURO

The Aprilia SMV750 Dorsoduro is the latest in a small number of road-legal motorcycles taking their inspiration from the Supermoto form of motorcycle racing - essentially motocross, or "dirt", bikes fitted with slick road racing tyres and raced over a half-tarmac/half-dirt circuit.

The lightweight, agile, and powerful Dorsoduro is driven by a new generation of engine incorporating the most advanced technical solutions found on any bike of its kind. Thanks to advanced electronic engine management, Aprilia's compact 90° V twin delivers superb performance, well beyond the reach of its rivals. Specific power is 122.6 HP/litre and maximum torque is 82 Nm at only 4,500 rpm.

The concept that revolutionised the world of Supermoto has now engendered the Aprilia Dorsoduro 750. This unique, elite motorcycle applies all of Aprilia's vast racing experience to just one mission: the offer of pure riding enjoyment. 92 HP and exclusive Tri-Map ride-by-wire technology mean that the lightweight and powerful Dorsoduro 750 can satisfy even the most expert riders in search of a state-of-the-art motorcycle.

Italian manufacturer Aprilia has a long and successful racing history in Supermoto. The concept suits Aprilia's desired corporate image as performance-related but not ordinary. The Dorsoduro was the company's first attempt to transfer that race pedigree to road bike sales.

APRILLIA SHIVER

From everyday use to a trip along mountain passes or use on the racetrack, the Aprilia Shiver 750 is completely at home in any situation, guaranteeing pure riding pleasure at all times.

The Aprilia Shiver 750 is the first ever production motorcycle equipped with integral ride-by-wire electronic throttle control. Thanks to this advanced system, the Aprilia V90 engine delivers an exceptional power output for its size and configuration. Maximum power of 95 HP at 9,000 rpm and maximum torque of 81 Nm at 7,000 rpm are incredible figures for an engine of this displacement. Impressive torque, already available at low revs, makes riding the Shiver 750 on country roads an amazing experience.

Light, agile and powerful, it has a latest generation engine and the most advanced technical features in its class. The 90° V2 produced entirely in-house by Aprilia is extremely compact. Above all, thanks to the advanced electronic management, it can deliver a level of power comparable to four cylinder engines in the same class, but with much more favourable torque at low revs for an efficient and pleasing ride even on everyday routes. True to the Aprilia tradition, the chassis simply has no rivals in its class. The mixed steel trellis and aluminium side plate frame provides standard setting rigidity. All this makes the bike extremely compact and the perfect ride for beginner and expert alike.

BMW K1300S

The latest version of BMW's rocketship K1300S has had a host of small changes that add up to a much better bike all round. With a claimed 175bhp and some seriously clever electronically-adjustable suspension, traction control and a long list of options to choose from, BMW has built a bike that can handle almost everything. And don't forget the new K-series range now has proper indicators rather than the confusing triple switches of old. The motor is the biggest single area of improvement. Engineering development was handed over to the spanner magicians at Ricardo – the same firm that designed the gearbox for the 1000bhp Bugatti Veyron hypercar. This is the first time BMW has worked with Ricardo on one of its bikes. The result is a claimed 175bhp from an increased 1293cc four-cylinder motor that is much smoother with bundles of power and torque. It's one of the best big-capacity motors on the road today combining lovely refinement with a racing engine snarl when pushed. The K1300S is a big bike – with a 228kg dry weight, it is never going to be a race-designed lightweight. However, the clever Electronic Suspension Adjustment (ESA II) system does a great job of hiding that weight. The suspension has nine potential settings to cover solo riding, pillion and both settings with luggage.

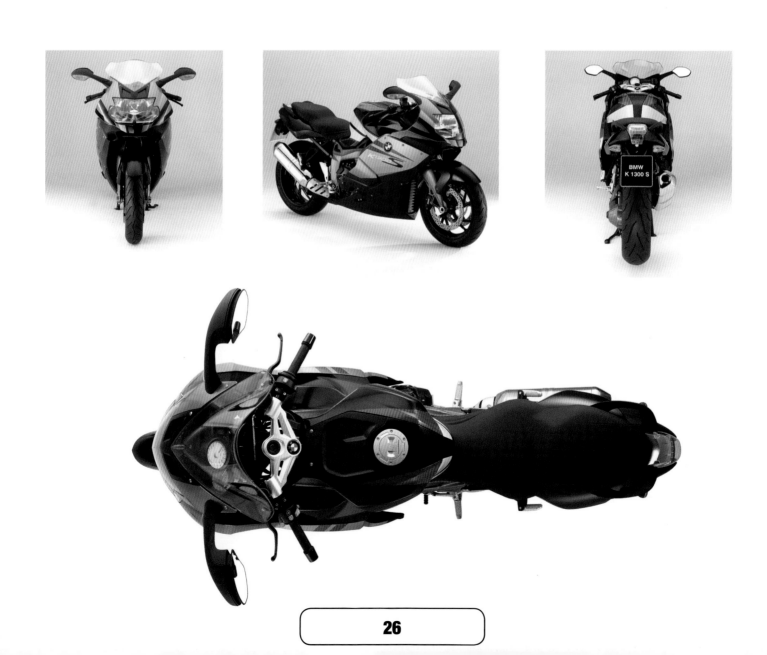

BMW S1000RR

The BMW S1000RR is a super bike manufactured by BMW Motorrad to compete in the 2009 Superbike World Championship. It was introduced in Munich on 16 April 2008, and is powered by a 999 cc (60.9 cu in) inline-4 engine redlined at 14,200 rpm.

BMW will only manufacture 1,000 production models in 2009 to satisfy World Superbike homologation requirements. It features traction control, has an overall wet weight (motorcycle) of 204 kg (450 lb) . The S1000RR is unlikely to be in dealerships until early 2010. A massive 193 horsepower is just the beginning - the S1000RR packs a combined ABS that's lighter and smarter than Honda's, variable intake tracts and exhaust butterflies that outdo the Yamaha and MV Agusta systems, a 4-mode variable engine mapping system that seems a lot better thought-out than Suzuki's, and a very clever traction control system that's integrated into the mind-boggling fly-by-wire engine management system in a way that seems much more logical than Ducati's.

On 26 June 2008, Spanish rider Ruben Xaus signed to ride the bike for the factory BMW Motorrad team. On 25 September 2008, Australian former double Superbike World Champion Troy Corser signed to complete the team's two-rider lineup for 2009.

As of May 2009, in the 2009 Superbike World Championship season, the highest race result achieved by Corser is 8th place in the opening round in Australia, and Xaus achieved 7th place in Italy.

BMW R1200 GS

For the hearty adventure-touring types, the R1200GS Adventure returns with a few updates aimed at smoothing out the riding experience a bit. The most notable addition is the inclusion of the Enduro ESA (Electronic Suspension Adjustment). This means that the chassis can be set up for the current riding conditions and load at the touch of a button, with adjustable damper settings and suspension height on both wheels. As a result, the suspension has the travel to prevent bottoming out on rough ground, but still delivers optimum roadholding in everyday use. Other updates include two-piece hand guards, a taller windscreen and a claimed 5% boost in power. An adjustable seat and optional ABS are standard fare on BMW bikes these days but the 8.7-gallon fuel tank, assortment of crash protectors and knobby tires give the Adventure the ability to get the bike deep into unchartered territory and back again. The short first gear option is exclusive to the R 1200 GS Adventure, and reduces the already-low creep speed by a further 10 per cent, something which is particularly useful over broken ground in tight spaces. Because control is every bit as important as power – especially in the sort of terrain that other bikes can't even reach in the first place. Other optional extras include ASC (Automatic Stability Control) and TPC (Tyre Pressure Control).

After four years, the R1200GS gets a few nip/tuck cosmetic enhancements, starting with stainless steel knee covers on both sides of the gas tank, which should provide additional protection from the elements. Both the fork tubes and cylinder head covers have also received some 'sporty' design treatments to go along with the new five-spoke wheels.

BMW G 650 X CHALLENGE

Powered by a 652cc Single, the new G 650 X represents the lightest-powered machines in the BMW inventory. A constant on all three versions is the single-cylinder powerplant, now claimed to be 4.5 lbs lighter than the earlier 650 engine.

All three 650s sport a bridge frame constructed out of tubular steel with cast aluminum sections to the side and an aluminum rear frame bolted on. An aluminum-alloy double swingarm rounds out the skeletal design. A 2.1-gallon fuel tank is positioned within the frame triangle beneath the seat, a carryover from the F650 design, and provides an operating range of 155 miles.

The Xchallenge uses a 21-inch front wheel combined with an 18-inch rear, both spoked with aluminum rims and hubs, and accommodate standard 90/90-21 and 140/80-18 off-road meat. A 300mm wave disc teams with a double-piston floating caliper to take care of braking duties up front, while a 240mm rotor (also waved) is grabbed by a single-piston floater out in the back. The Xchallenge is unique to its two 650 siblings with a shorter final drive ratio, via its 15-tooth pinion and 47-tooth sprocket.

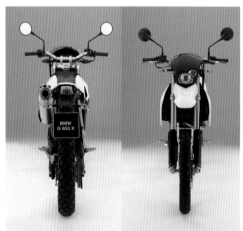

BUELL 1125CR

The Buell 1125R is a super bike manufactured by Buell. It is powered by a 1125 cc Helicon V-twin engine produced by Rotax (or BRP-Rotax) of Austria. This liquid-cooled engine has a V angle of 72 degrees and produces a reported 146 hp (109 kW), with a maximum rpm limit of 10,500.

The 72 degree included angle in this engine is a change from previous V-twins from this manufacturer which are 90° (Ducati, Suzuki, Aprilia) or 60° (Aprilia, Can-Am), or 45° (Harley-Davidson Evolution) engines. Voxan is also using 72° V-twins.

The 1125r includes a number of unique design attributes. The patented frame design houses the bikes' fuel. The single, 8 piston front brake features a large, inverted rotor that is directly attached to the bike's front rim. This feature allows Buell to design a lighter, more responsive front end than traditional designs. The bike also utilizes an exhaust under the engine for greater volume. For the 2009 model year, Buell introduced the 1125CR, a version of the 1125R in the cafe racer style The Intuitive Response Chassis (IRC) is the stiffest ever built, resulting in a bike that's better able to hold a line with minimal flexing or bending. Constructed of lightweight aluminium, it responds with precision and predictability during aggressive riding, delivering an unprecedented amount of feedback, regardless of road conditions.

BUELL LIGHTNING® CITYX XB9SX

With its 1320mm wheelbase, the Lightning handles with surgical precision. The 21-degree rake and 83.8mm trail improves agility. The aluminium frame is both lightweight and incredibly rigid, improving the bike's stability in corners. By housing the 14.5 litres of fuel, it also lowers the centre of gravity, making it feel light and flickable. The Zero Torsional Load (ZTL™) Braking System consists of a 375 mm rotor mounted to the wheel's perimeter and a 6-piston caliper. When applied, it transfers braking forces (a.k.a. torsional load) directly to the rim instead of through the spokes. Without the need for load-bearing spokes or even a second disc, the bike's front end weighs in about 2.5Kg lighter than what you'd find on most dual disc set-ups. Fully adjustable, 43 mm Showa® inverted fork features a high performance damping cartridge that lets you adjust the set up for any situation. Whether it's at the track or the ride home, you can optimise the suspension for excellent feedback and razor sharp handling. When combined with the adjustable rear shock, it's the most tunable suspension in the business. The Thunderstorm® 984 cc, 45-degree V-Twin delivers the iconic look, thunderous sound, and power-pulsing feel that only an V-Twin engine can offer. Following the style of an American Muscle machine, you can tap into maximum torque in any gear, regardless of where the tach needle is pointing. In fact, you'll find that over 85% of the motor's torque is available at just 2500 RPMs. Performance and dependability are enhanced with a large crank pin, a large capacity oiling system, and an electronic timing system and ECM that controls a DDFI 3 fuel injection system. Combined, these features improve drivability and performance, and reduce service maintenance costs.

BUELL LIGHTNING XB12SS

With a 53.7-inch wheelbase, the Lightning Long XB12Ss offers an expanded cockpit for the rider, a larger passenger position and 4.4-gallon fuel-in-frame capacity for extended range. For 2009, the suspension is upgraded to offer the supermoto-like handling previously found on the Lightning Super TT, with front and rear travel extended to 5.6 inches. A new, sculpted Streetfighter saddle maintains seat height at 30.6 inches and covers a handy storage compartment. The new Buell ZTL2 eight-piston front caliper enhances braking performance.The Thunderstorm® 1203 cc, 45-degree V-Twin delivers the iconic look, thunderous sound, and power-pulsing feel that only an V-Twin engine can offer. Following the style of an American Muscle machine, you can tap into maximum torque in any gear, regardless of where the tach needle is pointing. In fact, you'll find that over 85% of the motor's torque is available at just 2500 RPMs. Performance and dependability are enhanced with a large crank pin, a large capacity oiling system, and an electronic timing system and ECM that controls a DDFI 3 fuel injection system. Combined, these features improve drivability and performance, and reduce service maintenance costs. The Lightning Long is available with Midnight Black, Cherry Bomb Translucid, or Hero Blue Translucid bodywork.

DUCATI 1198S

The new Superbike range presents five models: The lightweight and agile 848, the awesomely powerful new 1198, and for those who demand the ultimate in specification, the 1198 S and 1098 R, both now with race-level Ducati Traction Control systems for the road. To mark his 3rd Superbike World Championship and to celebrate the career of Troy Bayliss, who will now retire from motorcycle racing, Ducati will build a 1098 R Bayliss Limited Edition.

The Ducati Traction Control (DTC) system further underlines Ducati's technology flow from racing to production and demonstrates how solutions developed for the track can be applied to enhance safety on the road. The Ducati 848, 1198 and 1098 R Superbikes are the most advanced, most powerful twin-cylinder motorcycles ever built. They are the product of a team of designers and engineers who have combined their Ducati MotoGP and World Superbike technologies to create the finest sport bikes in the world. From race-level engine specifications to world championship-winning traction control, the results are pure excellence. The 1198 uses engineering solutions taken directly from the World Championship winning 'R' model of Troy Bayliss. From engine capacity and specification to advanced electronics, many details that helped Troy to the 2008 World Superbike title have been applied to the 2009 road-going 1198.

HARLEY DAVIDSON IRON 883

The Iron 883 or XL 883 N is a new sportster model added to Harley Davidsons 2009 line up. The Iron 883 provides responsive handling, smooth clutch effort and durable carbon reinforced drive belt while pushing the styling of motorcycling minimalism to the edge. Decked in black from fender-to-fender, the new Harley-Davidson Iron 883 motorcycle brings the beat of an 883 Evolution engine backed up by a combo of gritty, old-school garage features like front fork gaiters, drag style handlebar and side-mount license plate holder.

The black powder-coated 883cc Evolution powertrain with black covers takes the Iron 883 motorcycle deep into the heart of darkness. With Electronic Sequential Port Fuel Injection (ESPFI) and performance tuning with a broad torque curve, the Iron 883 delivers plenty of power for the city scene. The pipes on the straight cut shorty dual exhaust flow the distinctive Harley-Davidson V-Twin sound. A classic solo seat with a height of 25.3 inches fits the lone rider, while a passenger seat and a backrest in complementing black finishes can be added as accessories.

HARLEY DAVIDSON XR1200

The XR 1200 is a powerful new Harley-Davidson hot rod motorcycle that was initially designed and launched only in European markets in April 2008. Inspired by the XR-750, the most dominating American dirt track racing motorcycle of all-time, the Harley-Davidson XR 1200 is now poised to boost adrenalin levels on streets, roads and highways around the world. The 1200 cc Evolution V-Twin engine with its high 10.0:1 compression ratio, performance cams, downdraft fuel injection, precision-cooled cylinder heads and large capacity oil cooler cranks out high torque. Rubber mounted to a new frame with a cast aluminum swingarm, the engine delivers exhilarating performance and responsive handling with less vibration. A unique upswept, high-volume 2-1-2 straight shot exhaust system includes dual mufflers and is finished in satin chrome. Motorcyclist featured the XR1200 on the cover of its July 2008 issue, and was generally positive about it in their "First Ride" story, in which Harley-Davidson was repeatedly asked to sell it in the United States. The XR1200 was released in the United States in 2009, in a special color scheme including Mirage Orange highlighting its dirt-tracker heritage.

The XR1200 borrows heavily from the XR-750 line of motorcycles which have been in production since 1959. The first 750 XR1200 models in 2009 were pre-ordered and came with a number 1 tag for the front of the bike, autographed by Kenny Roberts and Scott Parker and a thank you/welcome letter from Harley-Davidson, signed by Bill Davidson.

HARLEY DAVIDSON VRSCF V-ROD

The wide, angular air-box cover and chopped tail section look as solid and smooth as billet and give the new V-Rod Muscle lines that are clean and powerful. The size of the massive 240 mm rear tire is accentuated by the new broad, clipped and clean rear fender. The combination stop/tail/turn LED light is tucked under the edge of the rear fender, and the side-mount license plate leaves the fender surface smooth and uncluttered. Front-end styling balances the rear, with a trimmed fender that's blacked out behind satin-finished inverted forks and LED turn signals integrated into the mirror stems. The radiator shrouds are restyled and color-matched to the rest of the bodywork, while the new airbox side covers incorporate air scoop inlets covered with woven wire mesh. The silver five-spoke cast aluminum front and rear wheels are a new design for the V-Rod line.

A new deep seat holds the rider firmly in place against the thrust of the Revolution V-Twin engine. The Muscle features forward foot controls, and a new handlebar with internal wiring. The handlebar is 1.5-inch cast aluminum with tubular steel ends and integrated risers. Bold polished forged aluminum triple clamps secure the inverted forks and frame the distinctive V-Rod teardrop reflector optic headlamp, housed in a satin black bucket.

The long profile of a 34-degree fork rake is stretched visually by new "sidepipe" dual exhausts in satin chrome with fat, turn-out mufflers exiting behind the rear axle. The V-Rod Muscle is available in Vivid Black, Brilliant Silver, Dark Blue Denim and Red Hot Sunglo.

HONDA CBR 1000 RR

The CBR1000RR (also known as the Fireblade) is a 999 cc (60.9 cu in) liquid-cooled inline four-cylinder Honda sport bike that was introduced in 2004 to replace the CBR954RR.

The Honda CBR1000RR was developed by the same team that was behind the Honda RC211V race bike for the MotoGP series. Many of the new technologies introduced in the Honda CBR600RR, a direct descendant of the RC211V, were used in the new CBR1000RR such as a lengthy swingarm, Unit Pro-Link rear suspension, and Dual Stage Fuel Injection System (DSFI).

An all new CBR1000RR was introduced at the Paris International Motorcycle Show on 28 September, 2007 for the 2008 model year. The CBR1000RR is powered by an all new 999 cc (60.9 cu in) inline-four engine with a redline of 13,000 rpm. It features titanium valves and an enlarged bore with a corresponding reduced stroke. The engine has a completely new cylinder block, head configuration, and crankcase with lighter pistons. On the 5th of September 2008 Honda released details of the 2009 model. The bike remained the same, in terms of engine, styling and performance.

HONDA FURY

Featuring chopper styling cues such as the high headpipe and the largely exposed backbone frame tube, the Fury is Honda's attempt at creating a mass-produced "custom" chopper.

First seen in public today at the IMS show in New York, journalists got a sneak peek last month in American Honda's high-security R&D center in Torrance, CA. Company reps say customers want a "radical" looking chopper with Honda durability, quality, reliability and affordability.

The most expensive component of any motorcycle is its engine, so Honda was fiscally responsible and fitted a modified version of the 1312cc V-Twin seen in the VTX1300 variants. It retains the 52-degree Vee angle and single-pin crankshaft, but it differs in its cylinder heads, cams, port shapes and exhaust system. Most important is the addition of fuel-injection to the VTX's carbureted mill. We expect slight increases from the VTX's rear-wheel numbers of 59 hp and 71 ft-lbs of torque.

Like the VTX, the Fury has a five-speed transmission and utilizes a shaft-drive system. A color-matched aluminum swingarm with revised styling spices up the back end. Honda gave some consideration to using a belt-drive arrangement on the Fury, but it was cheaper to stick with what was already developed. There isn't one belt-driven bike in Honda's catalog. A 38.0-degree rake angle is quite chopperish, but it's balanced by a modest 3.5 inches of trail. At 71.2 inches, the Fury's wheelbase is the longest of any production Honda.

HONDA DN-01

The DN-01 (DN standing for "Dream New") is an entirely new category of motorcycle for Honda. Unvieled in concept form during the 39th annual Tokyo Motor Show in October 2005, it marked the beginning of a whole new category Honda calls "Crossover." Designed as a comfortable "Sports Cruiser", the DN-01 utilises a four valve 680cc 52° V-twin engine with a PGM-FI fuel injection system.

The bike uses an all new, hydromechanical automatic transmission called the HFT. The drive has an automatic and manual mode. In automatic mode, the rider has the option of two fully automatic transmission modes - "D" (Drive mode) for ordinary riding, and "S" (Sport mode) for sharper acceleration. In manual mode, the rider can make use of two simple left thumb operated buttons for shifting up or down the six-speed gear box. Riding the DN couldn't be easier. It's powered by a 680cc, 52-degree V-Twin borrowed from the European-market Transalp. Although it has roots to the late-1980s Hawk GT, the SOHC, 4-valve motor is thoroughly modernized with a sophisticated fuel-injection system using dual 40mm throttle bodies and high-tech 12-hole injectors.

KAWASAKI 650R

The Kawasaki Ninja 650R is the North-American-market name for the ER-6 introduced in 2006. The bike is a middleweight twin motorcycle, designed for normal use on paved roads. It has modern styling and features, with low-seating ergonomics, a low center of gravity, and respectable, manageable power output. Its design was intended to appeal to a wide-ranging audience from newcomers to seasoned riders. Kawasaki designed the 650R to maximize rider comfort and integration, and be aesthetically equivalent to larger, more powerful superbikes.

The 650R/faired ER-6, known as the ER-6f overseas, was introduced to the market in 2006 by Kawasaki Motorcycles. The unfaired ER-6n was not sold in North America until the 2009 model year. The motorcycle fits above the Ninja 250R & Ninja 500R models which already existed in Kawasaki's sportbike lineup, which includes the famous Ninja ZX models. For 2009, Kawasaki released an updated Ninja 650R which includes new bodywork, mirrors, gauges, lighting, and a new tune on the same 649 cc engine.

KAWASAKI NINJA ZX14

The Ninja ZX-14 (Kawasaki ZZR1400 in other territories) is a hyper sport motorcycle that is currently Kawasaki's most powerful sport bike. It was introduced at the 2005 Tokyo motor show and released for the 2006 model year as a replacement for the ZX-12R (manufactured through 2001-2006). Its direct competitor in the hyper sport segment is the Suzuki Hayabusa (GSX1300R). Secondary air ports in the cylinder head and its cover flow air quality in the exhaust system and increase the effectiveness of the three catalysts honeycomb work in the exhaust system. These devices, combined with wide dispersion of atomized fuel in the fine-atomizing fuel injectors and optimized flow characteristics through doses, allow the ZX-14 1352cc engine to offer a high performance, but still more difficult to meet emissions regulations for motorcycles. The ZX-14 chassis is every bit the equal of its power. Using an advanced version of Kawasaki unique aluminum monocoque design, its frame is lightweight and very strong. The cast aluminum sections on the main framework for lighter parts, maintenance even more weight on the thin and compact chassis.

The Ninja ZX-14 is capable of accelerating from 0–60 mph in 2.5 seconds with the top speed being electronically limited to 186 mph (299 km/h). This limit has been in effect on both Kawasaki and Suzuki sport motorcycles since 2001 when both companies realized that the speed arms race between the two companies would only serve to bring about government regulation. However, it has been reported that the Ninja is capable of speeds in excess of 210 mph with its limiter removed after an aftermarket modification.

KAWASAKI VERSYS

Kawasaki introduced the Versys, a middleweight motorcycle with a standard riding posture, to the European and Canadian markets at the end of 2006, and to the US market in 2007. The name Versys is a combination of the words "versatile" and "system," suggesting a fusion of riding attributes intended to offer versatility.

Based on the Ninja 650R (ER-6 in Europe and Asia), the bike's 650 cc liquid cooled 4-stroke parallel twin engine has been retuned for more bottom-end and mid-range torque.

Compared to the ER-6, the Versys has a redesigned sub-frame, new exhaust header design, and redesigned suspension. The Versys replaces the standard non-adjustable suspension of the ER-6 with an inverted front fork featuring greater travel and adjustable for preload and rebound damping. The rear uses an alloy swingarm instead of the tubular steel item on the original bike.

The Versys' alloy wheels, ZR rated tires, and low, exposed exhaust system are poorly suited to off-road travel. Instead, the bike's specification follows closely that of its primary market competitor, the Suzuki DL650 V-Strom.

KAWASAKI NINJA ZX10R

A fearsome 998cc, four-cylinder engine that offers a strong mid-range punch followed by an eye-watering high-rpm crescendo. Part of the motor's success is its efficient respiratory system – the bank of four 43mm Keihin throttle bodies with oval sub-throttles. Controlled by Kawasaki's digital fuel injection (DFI®) system and featuring two injectors per cylinder, the throttle bodies utilize the airbox's efficient design to maximize flow for improved cylinder filling and maximum power output. On par with the impressive intake side, the equally efficient exhaust system lets the engine exhale with ease, while generating less noise and minimizing emissions. An excellent power delivery demands a top-notch transmission and the ZX-10R's is no exception. With gearing optimized to match the engine output, the transmission and engine are essentially a race-ready team with performance similar to Kawasaki's factory Superbikes. More racing heritage is found in its adjustable slipper clutch, which allows riders to dole out quick downshifts without upsetting the fine-tuned chassis.

The ZX-10R also has the Kawasaki Ignition Management System (KIMS) to enhance the precision with which the engine reacts to throttle changes. The KIMS works to prevent engine and catalyzer damage from sudden spikes in engine speed, providing a smooth and controlled throttle response to the rider. The system works by monitoring the standard DFI system's input data (engine speed, throttle position, vehicle speed, gear position and feedback from intake air temperature, intake air pressure, engine temperature and O_2 sensors), and checking every 0.02 seconds for any sudden changes in RPM. It doesn't interfere with normal operation and still allows the engine to rev freely under typical riding conditions.

MOTO GUZZI 1200 SPORT 4V

The throbbing heart of the 1200 SPORT 4V is the new "Quattrovalvole" (four valve) engine that, thanks to its unmistakeable transverse V90 architecture, cannot fail but to catch the eye. As the latest form of the engine that was fitted to the Griso and Stelvio, the "Quattrovalvole" on the 1200 SPORT 4V differs in its intake and exhaust system. These factors were developed to offer better engine response at medium to high revs and to match the sporting character of the bike. The engine puts out over 105CV at 7500 rpm with 110Nm of torque at 6500 rpm. The engine also acts as a load-bearing component of the tubular twin cradle frame. The frame itself is made of high resistance steel that provides solidity and rigidity.

In true Moto Guzzi tradition, only the best brakes and suspension systems are used: Brembo Gold Series brakes and Marzocchi forks grace the front end. The brakes have radial mounted four-piston calipers acting on 320 mm discs while the forks are a traditional 45 mm unit. The comfortable, excellent riding position along with the forward position of the handlebars give the rider complete control and allow him to concentrate on enjoying the ride.

The 1200 SPORT 4V is now available in the classic black or in the original titanium grey colour scheme. Both these schemes perfectly offset the white racing number plates on the screen and on the saddle that is edged with a subtle green, white and red stripe that celebrates the bike's Italian heritage.

MOTO GUZZI CAFÉ CLASSIC

In 1969 the Mandello del Lario mechanics increased the cubic capacity of their transverse 90° V engine from 703 to 757cc which greatly increased the level of maximum performances without in any way diminishing the notorious reputation of reliability and sturdiness that was behind the success of the V7 in the market and with the police forces of half the world. Designing the new Cafe Classic was given to Lino Tonti, one of the most brilliant Italian designers who, using the generous forms of the 750cc engine, built a highly streamline CrMo tubular frame. Low, long and hunched over the suspensions, the V7 Sport made its first appearance in the market with a rather unusual chromatic combination, obtained with the "Legnano" green used for the upper structures contrasting with the red frame of the first 150 specimens assembled in the Moto Guzzi testing department using a CrMo tubular frame as well as some changes to distribution and ignition details with respect to the next versions which had a black coloured frame. Boasting an excellent dynamic performance, the V7 Sport impressed the public and critics alike for being the first mass produced bike in the world able to exceed the maximum speed of 200 km/h and this fact was worthy of a report in 1972 by a renowned Italian motorbike magazine. Symbol of the "Italian style" sports bike, all substance and no frills, the V7 Sport magically reappears today in the distinct lines of the new V7 Cafè Classic. The similarities with its renowned ancestor blend together in the excellence of its dynamic performance and in the class of the stylistic features common to both, like the "Legnano" green of the upper structures, the rich chromings, the slanted half-handlebars, the instrument cockpit and other details that are unmistakably Moto Guzzi.

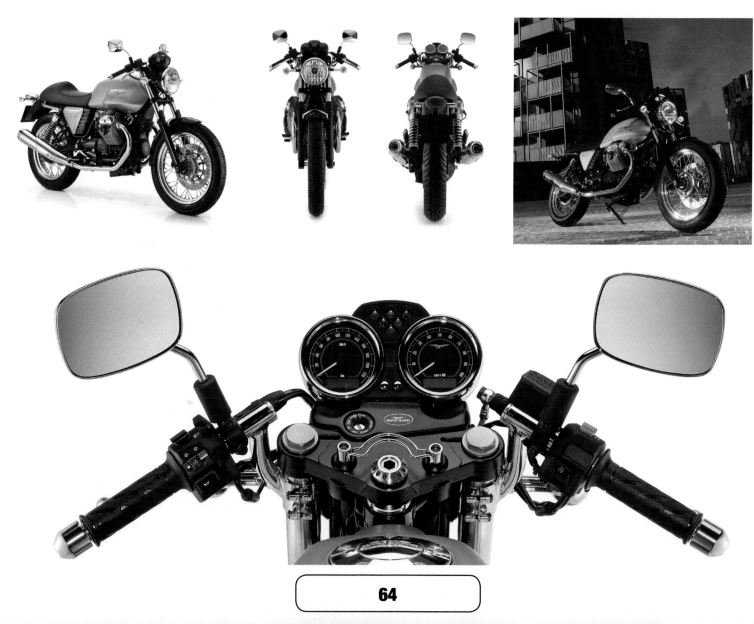

MOTO GUZZI GRISO 8V

The Griso 8V is Moto Guzzi's flagship "naked" motorcycle, manaufactured since 2006. Designed along classic lines the Griso features a powerful 1200cc modern 90° V-twin "Quattrovalvole" series engine. This engine develops a peak power of approximately 110 hp at just 7500 rpm.

The Griso's non conformist styling creates a rather strong and powerful looking bike. Featuring details made from the highest quality materials such as the premium leather upholstered saddle with visible stitching and spoked wheels to the aggressive looking twin-coiled exhaust which creates a stylistically pleasing figure-of-eight cross section.

Unvieled in September 2006 the "Quattrovalvole" engine is the most powerful production engine that is currently made by Moto Guzzi. The engine has a single overhead camshaft which operates 4 valves for each of the two cylinders. Theoretically the engine can push the bike well in excess of 140 mph. Designed to respect a tradition that has lasted forty years, the new engine adopts the rational 90° transverse V twin layout but with 563 new parts, and introduces for the first time single overhead cam valve timing and silent running Morse chains to operate the four valves per cylinder. 75% of this highly developed Moto Guzzi 1200 cc engine has been modified compared to its predecessor, to produce 110 HP at only 7500 rpm and a maximum torque of 11 Kgm at 6400 rpm.

MOTO GUZZI V7 CLASSIC

The V7 Classic is a retro themed motorcycle introduced in 2007 for the 2008 model year. Based loosely on the original 70s V7 machine Moto Guzzi has brought it fully up-to-date with its equipment levels, frame engineering and 750cc Euro 3 engine.

Famed for its reliability and low consumption, the 744 cc 90° V twin 744 cc (bore and stroke - 80 mm by 74 mm) houses special graphite low wear pistons and aluminium alloy cylinders.

The small block from Mandello is fed by an electronic Weber Marelli fuel injection system with 36 mm throttle bodies and a Lambda probe that puts the engine firmly into the Euro 3 homologation category. The five-speed gearbox is precise with neutral easy to find and the ratios have been chosen for touring purposes.

It has a maximum torque of 54.7 Nm comes in at only 3600 rpm. That doesn't mean poor acceleration however as the maximum power output of nearly 50 CV is synchronised to perfection with the characteristics of the V7 Classic. This bike has no need to race against the clock, it just has to enjoy itself. Like every Moto Guzzi, the booming sound from the V twin says it all.

MOTO GUZZI NORGE 1200

The Norge 1200 is Moto Guzzi's GT (Gran Turismo) motorcycle, that has been in production since the 2005 model year. It derives its name from the original GT Norge famous for making a grueling 4,000-mile (6,400 km) test ride in 1928 —from the company headquarters in Mandello del Lario, Italy to Lapland, just inside the Arctic Circle of Norway's Capo Nord — to prove its suspension prototype: the world's first rear swingarm suspension. The elastic frame with rear suspension was so successful that it was introduced in production machines and the G.T. was renamed the 'Norge' in memory of that unprecedented feat. Moto Guzzi celebrated the 2005 Norge introduction by re-tracing the 1928 raid. Reinforcing Moto Guzzi's history, the design of the Norge and its fairing was refined in the company's historic wind tunnel (the first of kind in the world) at the Mandello del Lario headquarters. The Norge 1200 is driven by Moto Guzzi's 90° V-Twin engine, that has a displacement of 1151cc, delivering 95HP at 7,500 rpm. The aim of the 'Norge project' is to offer all motorcyclists the chance to choose from a range of subtly but significantly different models, all of which offer a superb level of finish down to the smallest detail. What all models have in common, of course, is that exceptional Norge 1200 personality, elegant dynamic design, ergonomic controls and riding position, comfortable rider and passenger seat and short wheelbase for superior agility. Even though your riding is not all long distance touring, you still need proper safety equipment. The Norge 1200's ABS braking system provides precisely that, even on slippery surfaces. The Norge 1200 T has everything you need to travel in comfort in town and country alike, but if you want more, there is also a wide range of accessories to extend your range of action.

SUZUKI GSX R1300 HAYABUSA

With performance credentials that establish it as the hottest sportbike on the planet, the Suzuki Hayabusa is designed for serious sport riders who will settle for nothing less than the best. Its combination of unsurpassed power, crisp handling and superb aerodynamics creates the ultimate sportbike. The 1340cc, DOHC liquid-cooled engine with 16-valves, Twin Swirl Combustion Chambers provides 11% higher performance and smoother operation. High efficiency curved radiator now features dual electric fans controlled by the ECM for increased cooling capacity. Oil cooler now has 10 rows cores for increased heat dissipation. Ion plating treatment utilizing PVD (physical vapor deposit) method is applied to piston rings providing a smoother surface treatment for increased durability, reduced friction loss and reduced oil consumption. Large volume 4-2-1-2 exhaust system with a large capacity catalyzer, dual triangular canisters and closed loop system that meets Euro 3 and Tier 2 regulations. Lightweight aluminum alloy pistons feature a revised shape and a higher compression ratio of 12.5:1 for maximum performance in all conditions. Lightweight titanium intake and exhaust valves with narrow 14 degree valve angle for high combustion chamber efficiency. SCEM (Suzuki Composite Electro-chemical Material) plated cylinders minimize cylinder size and improve heat dissipation and new hydraulic cam chain tensioner for reduced mechanical noise. S-DMS (Suzuki Drive Mode Selector) allows the rider to choose from three different engine settings depending on riding conditions or rider preferences. Slick shifting 6 speed transmission working in conjunction with an innovative back torque limiting clutch for smooth and controlled downshifts.

SUZUKI GSX R1000

The GSX-R1000 is a super bike from Suzuki's GSX-R series of motorcycles. It was introduced in 2001 to replace the GSX-R1100 and is powered by a liquid-cooled 999 cc (61.0 cu in) inline four-cylinder 4-stroke engine.

The GSX-R1000 engine was a redesigned GSX-R750 engine. The R1000 had a 1 mm (0.039 in) bigger bore and 13 mm (0.51 in) longer stroke, newly designed pistons with lower crown, and gear-driven counter balancer. The performance of the engine is a peak of 160 bhp at 9,500 rpm as measured on the crank and 143hp when measured on the rear wheel with small variations between different instances of the same model, the redline is set at 12,000 rpm.

On 22 September, 2006, Suzuki revealed a significantly updated GSX-R1000 for 2007 at the Paris motor show. The new bike gained 14 lb (6.4 kg) over the 2006 model which was due to its new exhaust system and new emissions regulations. To counter this significant weight increase, Suzuki claimed improved aerodynamics. It also featured three different engine mapping configurations, selectable via a three-position handlebar switch; standard, sport, and 'wet'.

As the newly crowned AMA Superbike Championship series winner — for an incredible sixth straight year — the Suzuki GSX-R1000 is the undisputed dominant superbike of our era. For 2009, it's making history in another way: it's totally redesigned for even greater racetrack performance.

SUZUKI BOULEVARD M109R

A streamlined headlight cover carrying a unique trapezoidal shaped multi reflector H4 halogen headlight and a maintenance free LED tail light built into the tailsection. 1783cc, 8-valve DOHC, 54 degree, liquid-cooled, fuel injected V-twin engine designed for strong throttle response and quick acceleration. A compact dry sump lubrication system SASS (Suzuki Advanced Sump System) provides reduced engine height, a lower crankshaft position and lower center of gravity. A new Idle Speed Control (ISC) system improves cold starting and stabilizes engine idle speed in various conditions. Dual spark plug per cylinder ignition system is controlled by the powerful 32 bit ECM for improved combustion efficiency and reduced exhaust emissions. Each bore is lined with Suzuki's race proven SCEM (Suzuki Composite Electrochemical Material) for optimum heat transfer, tighter piston-to-cylinder clearances and reduced weight. Electronic fuel injection system features the Suzuki Dual Throttle Valve system (SDTV) with 56mm throttle bodies - maintains optimum air velocity for smooth low- to mid-range throttle response. Five speed transmission features carefully selected gear ratios for comfortable cruising in a variety of riding situations. Massive 112mm bore and 90.5mm stroke utilizing huge 112mm forged aluminum alloy pistons with short skirts, and cut away sides riding on chrome moly steel connecting rods. The 2-into-1-into-2 stainless steel chromed exhaust system features Suzuki's digitally controlled SET (Suzuki Exhaust Tuning) system for optimum engine performance and powerful V-twin sound.

SUZUKI B-KING

The B-King is a naked sport bike that was unveiled in 2007. It is based on the Hayabusa Hyper Sport bike (GSX1300R) and uses the same 1340 cc (81.7 cu in) engine, but with different exhaust and inlet systems. The bike was originally revealed in 2001 in concept form at the Tokyo Motor Show.

The engine in the B-King is an all new variation of the 1340cc, DOHC liquid-cooled, 16 valve found in the Hayabusa which produces a tested 162.97 hp (122 kW) and 85.72 lb·ft (116 N·m) of torque. The improved exhaust system features a lightweight titanium intake and valves with a narrow 14 degree angle for high combustion chamber efficiency. 32 bit ECU boasts 1024 ROM for high overall performance and to control new functions like S-DMS. High efficiency curved radiator now features dual electric fans controlled by the ECM for increased cooling capacity. Oil cooler now has 10 rows cores for increased heat dissipation. Ion plating treatment utilizing PVD (physical vapor deposit) method is applied to piston rings providing a smoother surface treatment for increased durability, reduced friction loss and reduced oil consumption. Large volume 4-into-2-into-1 exhaust system with a large capacity catalyzer, oxygen sensors and an oval cross section canister with dual openings that meets Euro 3 and Tier 2 regulation. Slick shifting 6 speed transmission working in conjunction with an innovative back torque limiting clutch for smooth and controlled downshifts

TRIUMPH AMERICA

The Triumph Bonneville America was launched in 2002 as a 'factory custom' cruiser, aimed at the important United States export market. The original model had the 790cc air-cooled DOHC twin engine and although based on the Bonneville was very different to ride with the wheelbase extended 6.4 inches to 65.2 inches, making it 6.8 inches longer overall. The saddle was lowered 2.2 inches and the steering head rake angle increased by 4.3 degrees giving a 33.3 degree rake. The America had the Bonneville's 12.2 inch front disc but the front wheel was reduced to 18 inches diameter and the rear wheel to 15 inches with a larger 11.2 inch disc brake. The America also had a larger fuel tank with a 'chromed' plastic console to house the filler, 4.5 inch diameter speedometer and warning lights.

In 2007 the engine capacity was increased to 865cc (carburated) delivering peak power at 6,800 rpm, with maximum torque of 74Nm available at 3,300rpm.

In 2008 the Bonneville America was further updated with a electronic fuel injection system to meet the European emission legislation, with the fuel injectors concealed by dummy carburetors.

TRIUMPH BONNEVILLE

New for 2009, the Bonneville gets an authentic 70's look that's sure to appeal to riders of all ages and experience. New 17" cast wheels sharpen the handling whilst the short front and rear mudguards, lower and narrower seat and upswept megaphone style silencers are pure 70's styling and give a fresh sportier look. Triumph launched the first new Bonneville for 15 years at the Munich Motorcycle Show in September 2000, with a 790 cc 360 degree crank parallel twin engine. The T100 Bonneville, styled by John Mockett and David Stride, was launched as an uprated version with a 865 cc engine fitted to all Bonnevilles from 2007. The designation comes from the top speed of 100 mph (160 km/h) and it is sold as part of Triumph's "Modern classics" range. The engine gives 67 bhp (50 kW) at 7,200rpm and features double electrically heated carburettors. Triumph added an air injection unit near the spark plug to achieve emission regulations introduced in 2007. For 2008 the T100 was further updated with fuel injection to meet new Euro 3 emissions legislation. As well as cleaner running than a carburettor engine, the fuel injected system is also easier to start from cold. To retain the 'retro' styling the fuel injectors are hidden behind throttle bodies designed to resemble carburettors.

TRIUMPH DAYTONA 675

Introduced in 2006, the Daytona 675 is a middleweight sport bike built by Triumph to replace the Daytona 650. The 2008 model has a tested dry weight of 389.4 lb (176.6 kg) and wet weight of 417 lb (189 kg). Tested power output is rated at 104.4 hp (78 kW) @ 12,100 rpm with 47 ft·lbf (64 N·m) @ 10,400 rpm.

The 2009 model of the Daytona has had over 50 technical inmprovements according to Triumph. While the only obvious change is that the front fairing has been changed slightly to improve aerodynamics and air flow, the new model is lighter, has 3 more horse power, the ECU has been remapped to extend first gear, and handling has improved through high and low speed dampers. The engine now has an increased power output, now up 3PS to 128PS peak, plus a 3 kg reduction in overall weight. The rear wheel has been reworked to reduce weight and inertia for quicker acceleration and improved suspension performance. The 2009 Daytona improves on this still further with new fully adjustable front and rear suspension, both of which allow the rider to adjust high and low speed compression damping separately.

There's further evidence of our ongoing performance focus with increased power output, now up 3bhp to 126bhp peak, plus a 7lb reduction in overall weight. The rear wheel has been reworked to reduce weight and inertia for quicker acceleration and improved suspension performance.

TRIUMPH ROCKET III

The Triumph Rocket III is a British motorcycle made by the Hinckley Triumph factory and has the largest displacement engine of any mass production motorcycle in the world (as of September 2008), at 2294 cc (139.9 cu in). The shaft driven Rocket III produces 200 Nm (150 ft·lbf) @ 2500 rpm and 140 bhp (100 kW) @ 6000 rpm. Despite its size and weight of 704 lb (319 kg) dry, it is described as having good balance and "light and easy steering" even at low speeds. The original model was released in 2004 and has remained in production with only minor modifications other than a change of engine colour from silver to black in 2006. This model was awarded Motorcycle Cruiser magazine's 2004 Bike of the Year, Motorcyclist's 2004 Cruiser of the Year, and Cruising Rider magazine 2005 Bike of the Year. In 2006 a black finish to the engine was introduced and new colour choices of Graphite and 'Scorched Yellow' were added to the original colours of Jet Black and Cardinal Red. Special edition 'Tribal' colour schemes of Caeruleus Blue Flame and Mulberry Red Tribal were also released at an extra cost of over £1000. The awe inspiring 2300cc triple cylinder power plant delivers arm wrenching torque via shaft drive for amazing acceleration and controllable power off the line and through the gears. It's the world's largest production motorcycle, but the real surprise is that it handles like a bike half its size thanks to the design intent from day one. Performance, handling and usability will always be at the heart of all our motorcycles and the legendary Rocket III proves it.

TRIUMPH SPEED TRIPLE

The Speed Triple is a series of motorcycles produced by the Triumph Motorcycle Company. In 1994 the reborn Triumph became one of the earliest adopters of a new style of motorcycle referred to as a Streetfighter. This new class of bike was essentially a modern sportbike or race replica motorcycle but without the aerodynamic plastic fairing.

In 2005 Triumph released its fourth generation Speed Triple. While this was not a redesign of the scale of the T509, there were many changes to the bike. The engine was still the venerable and reliable fuel injected engine used since 1997, but it had been increased in capacity to 1050 cc. Other engine modifications resulted in a claimed 129 horsepower (96 kW) and an even broader, flatter torque curve.

Late in 2007 a few changes appeared in the Speed Triple, consisting of an updated engine management system and a revised exhaust containing a catalytic converter in a different location. The revised Electronic Control Unit (ECU) had more memory and provided a solution for some starting and low speed fueling issues. Fitted with fully adjustable front and rear suspension, Nissin 4-piston radial front calipers and radial master cylinder, parts normally found in the supersports category.

YAMAHA FJR 1300A

The FJR1300 was introduced to Europe in 2001 before arriving in North America in 2002 with the 2003 model year designation and offered in a non-ABS version only. It had 298 mm front rotors.

The 2004 North American models included both a non-ABS version with traditional blue anodized brake calipers and a new ABS version. Other refinements included an upgrade to the suspension rates, 320 mm front brake rotors, and a fairing pocket for small items.

In 2006 the U.S. and World model years synchronized and design significantly changed including trailing arm changes, radiator curving, instrumentation changes, upgraded alternator and significant attention to airflow changes from reported heat issues in previous years.

For 2008 some minor changes were introduced, including an update to the altitude-related ECU issues and throttle 'feel', notably to improve low speed on/off throttle transitions. The colours announced in Europe are; Silver (Silver Tech), Black (Midnight Black) and Graphite. 2008 also sees minor changes in the ABS system. Equipped with a low-maintenance shaft drive, the 1,298cc inline 4-cylinder engine produces silky-smooth performance for an effortless ride – and with its adjustable windscreen, handlebars and seat – as well as heated grips and a 25-litre fuel tank – the FJR1300A is ready to cover enormous distances in deluxe sports style. And for added comfort, the 2009 model is equipped with a redesigned clutch with reduced load in the clutch lever operation.

YAMAHA FZ1

The Yamaha FZ1 is a street motorcycle that has been manufactured Yamaha since 2001. Yamaha also produces a smaller, similar 600cc version of this motorcycle called the FZ6. Models produced in the period 2001 to 2005 were known as FZS1000S (Fazer in Europe). They had a modified Yamaha YZF-R1 motor in a steel tubular frame. The FZ1 was carbureted and produced around 140 horsepower (108 to 111 True horsepower). In some European countries the 2005 model saw the introduction of an exhaust based catalytic converter, albeit of a rudimentary design.

2006 saw the introduction of a completely new model. The main changes included a new chassis, suspension, body work and a completely new engine, never seen before in the big Fazer. This brought the bike up to date with modern rivals. There have been instances of fuel injection glitches on the new model, although there are various 'fixes' available. The 2007 and on models have resolved most of these early fuel injection problems. The 2006 model has a 998 cc DOHC 20-valve R1 engine, which produces 150 crank horsepower (118 to 122 wheel horsepower)at 11,000 rpm, set in an all-new compact aluminum frame.

Its R1-based engine packs a mighty midrange punch and that cast aluminium frame cuts its way through the curves like a supersport bike, so whatever's going down on the street you're always in charge.

YAMAHA YZF-R1

Yamaha launched the YZF-R1 after redesigning the Genesis engine to offset the crankshaft, gearbox input and output shafts and this "compacting" of the engine yielded a huge dividend in that the total engine length was now very short. This allowed the wheelbase to be shortened significantly which resulted in much quicker handling and an optimized center of gravity. In late 2008 Yamaha announced they would release an all new R1 for 2009. The new R1 takes engine technology from the M1 Moto GP bike with its crossplane crankshaft, the first ever production motorcycle to do so. Crossplane technology, puts each connecting rod 90° from the next, with an uneven firing interval of 270°- 180°- 90°- 180°. The idea of this technology is to reduce internal crankshaft torque, thus giving the new R1 a more linear power delivery. Yamaha claims the bike would give the rider 'two engines in one', the low torque of a twin and the pace of an inline four. As with previous incarnations of the R1 the 2009 model keeps its YCC-T (Yamaha Chip Controlled Throttle). The R1 is now rated at 182 PS @ 12,500rpm at the crankshaft (without ram-air).

For 2009 this legendary motorcycle is equipped with an all-new 998cc inline four-cylinder engine with a crossplane crankshaft that runs with an uneven firing interval of 270° - 180° - 90° - 180°. This innovative new design ensures superb throttle linearity, giving a feeling that the rider's throttle hand is directly connected to the rear tyre. The new engine feels and sounds smoother than ever, and emits an unforgettable growl from the exhaust. Pushing out 182 PS at 12,500 rpm with 115.5 Nm of torque at 10,000 rpm

INDEX